P9-ARP-268

ZEN
baby

TO ELLEN + GLEN — 12/02
HAPPY HOLIDAYS + OUR BEST
WISHES FOR A JOYOUS NEW
YEAR! JOAND POSED FOR
YOU 1) IN A TREE
2) ON THE BEACH
3) ON THE BACK
COVER!
— CHECK IT OUT!
WITH ALL OUR
LOVE,
ROBERTA, NOAH +

ADAM
SACHS

ZEN baby

concept by Judith Adler

photographs by Paul Coughlin

clarkson potter/publishers
new york

Your children are not

your children.

They are the sons and daughters

of life's longing for itself.

—KAHLIL GIBRAN

INTRODUCTION

Zen Baby's vision is crystallized in the following true story: A two-and-a-half-year-old pestered his parents, masterfully of course, until they consented to his request *(demand)* to be left alone with his newborn brother. Over the nursery monitor, the parents overheard what it was the toddler had so insisted he needed to ask the new arrival. "Tell me again where we come from—I'm starting to forget." *Zen Baby* shares this wise tyke's thinking, looking to the original source of wisdom that reminds us to begin at the beginning, to see life through the eyes of Buddha-ful babies, with their souls wide open and ever ready to grace us with their grace.

"Beginner's mind," one of the most basic and profound Zen precepts, means bringing a clean slate, a pure mind, to everything we do. Whether we are stepping out on a new spiritual path, or have journeyed along one for lifetimes, the beginner's mind is something we all could do well to strive for. And what's so wonderful is that babies needn't strive for it, they *are* it, starting at the very beginning, each moment, each day, with every activity.

When I greet a baby fresh from heaven, I look right into his shining eyes, smile from my soul, and heartily welcome him to the planet, thank him for coming, and tell him I hope he enjoys his stay. After all, if he can make the immeasurable cosmic trip to arrive here, I certainly can find the time to express gratitude.

Zen teaches us to maximize our learning on this spin around the planet by choosing families we'll grow the most with—children pick their parents, parents pick their children, and siblings rival one another to figure out just who's to blame for picking one another. When parent(s) and child make a perfect fit, it's as if they instantly recognize they've chosen each other well and school's in session—the teacher is eager to teach, the student is ready to learn, and both are wise enough to know they'll spend their lives together switching places. An old adage says it all: A parent tells her child, "I'll teach you how to tie your shoes, you teach me everything else." The lessons we learn from babies far outweigh what we teach them. We learn generosity when they sweetly offer us their treasured teddy bear; joy when they give us the smile on their face; kindness when we watch them gently stroke a new puppy. Sure, little ones need their physical needs met—and they mean *now!*—but who wouldn't swap a first-tooth grin for a bowl of freshly smushed bananas?

Zen Baby marvels at the little Buddhas babies—bubbly in the bath, digging sand at the beach, or playing hide-and-seek with the camera. It wasn't hard to find subjects for *Zen Baby:* Any and all babies are Zen-like. Imagine the nourishment, both physical and emotional, an infant receives nursing at its mother's breast. Think back to the fluttering in your heart when you witnessed a child brave her first steps with focus and determination, or utter her first word to ecstatic parents who hear it as earth shattering as Bell heard Watson's first words over the telephone. Learning at the incredible speed babies do illustrates intelligence nothing short of Einstein, who wrote, "Every baby is born a genius." The key is holding the space for that pure genius to be respected, nurtured, and honored, helping him, and all of us, to hold on to the magic of babyhood forever. As Frank Lloyd Wright said, "Youth is a quality, and if you have it, you never lose it."

A MONK SAID: *What is this talk?*
THE MASTER SAID: *When I talk, you don't hear it.*
THE MONK SAID: *Do you hear it, sir?*
THE MASTER SAID: *Wait 'til I don't talk, then you hear it.*

Babies say everything without speaking a word. The twinkle in their eyes zings straight to our hearts with the speed of love. They peek mischievously into our souls. Not only do they hold *our* world in their hands, but they are also gracious enough to *share* their world with us. My heart beams with joy when I sit and watch a baby go off to her world, a place seekers have sought for lifetimes, somewhere close to where babies came from, a place, if we're lucky, we glimpse in our deepest meditation. Babies exist in that space—Zen means meditation, babies mean Zen. They don't need TV shows or movies—real life is the best show and everyday people are the greatest movie stars. Heck, they don't even need toys; the boxes they come in will do just fine.

I believe so deeply in the incredible spiritual power of babies, ones already on the planet and those waiting for physical bodies, that I wrote my own unborn children a letter. It welcomed them into my life and told them that while there's "womb" at my Soul's Inn, I'd prefer not to book a single room, rather a double suite, registered to their very own handpicked Mr. and Mrs. Mommy and Daddy. I suggested they use their powerful baby magic to go find Daddy, bring him to Mommy, and voilà—a ticket for the ride of their lives. And yet, somehow, by giving birth to this book, I feel closer to my own babies by way of feeling closer to all babies, having the honor of sharing such miraculous little spirits with the world.

> When Buddhists greet one another, we hold our palms together like a lotus flower, breathe in and out mindfully, bow, and say silently, "A lotus for you, a Buddha-to-be." This greeting produces two Buddhas at the same time.
>
> THICH NHAT HANH,
> BE STILL AND KNOW

When we see a baby's fresh face, it is like looking upon the Buddha himself, his smile a lotus flower, blooming before our very eyes. The radiance reminds us that we all are Buddhas-to-be, and that we can, in every moment, choose to remember what Buddha would do and, hopefully, actually do it.

Babies take us out of ourselves and, in exchange for insisting on our presence every moment, they give us back nothing short of everything they have to give. Many parents speak of the moment they first met their child as feeling they'd found a new, old friend, someone they'd spent lifetimes with and were honored to have found again. Looking into their beloved child's eyes, still cloudy with the clouds of heaven, they saw what every awake person sees: a three-way mirror showing us the very present, a reflection of our past, and an illumination of our future. I subscribe to the spiritual theory that says we are born knowing everything there is to know, and the challenge is not to forget it—because if we do, we'll be destined to spend the rest of our lives trying to find it again.

Each

individual is a

marvelous

opportunity.

—HIS HOLINESS THE DALAI LAMA

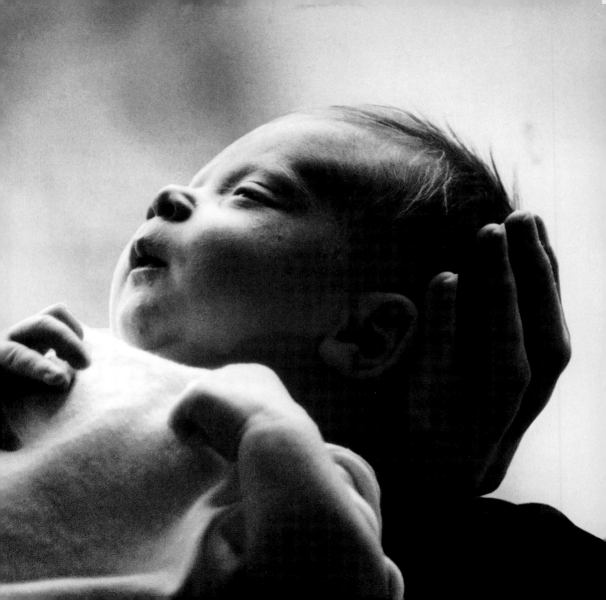

Wheresoever you go,
go with all your heart.

—CONFUCIUS

You have to

M E D I T A T E and *play,*

both at once.

—HIS HOLINESS THE DALAI LAMA

A musician must make his music,

An artist must paint,

A poet must write,

If he is to ultimately be at peace

with himself.

—ABRAHAM MASLOW

Scatter joy.

—RALPH WALDO EMERSON

To *chase* after Zen is like
chasing one's own shadow.

—ALAN WATTS

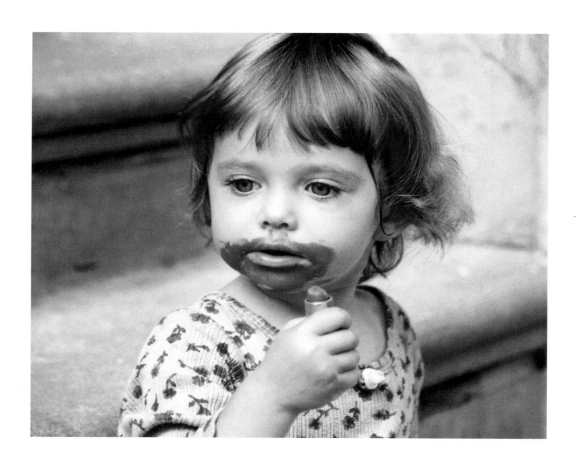

There is only one pretty child in the world,

and **every** *mother has it.*

—CHINESE PROVERB

Stick

to

one

task

until the end.

—HOZUMI GENSHO ROSHI,
ZEN HEART

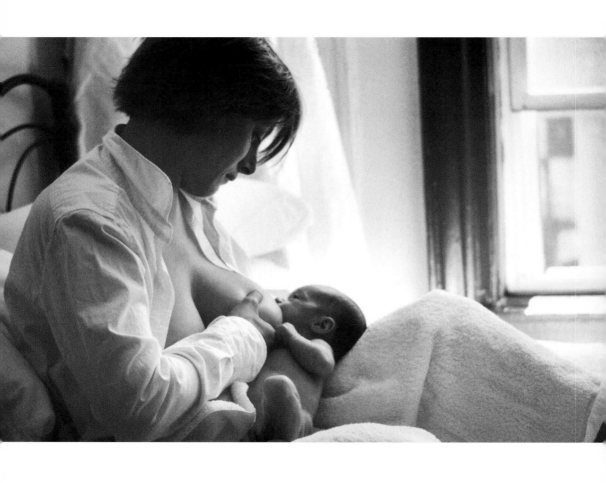

Wholesome spiritual nourishment

can be found looking at

the BLUE SKY,

the spring blossoms,

or the *eyes of a baby*.

We can celebrate the joys that are available

in these simple pleasures.

—THICH NHAT HANH,
BE STILL AND KNOW

ZEN is like **soap**;

first you wash with it,

then you

wash off the soap.

—ZEN SAYING, *365 ZEN*

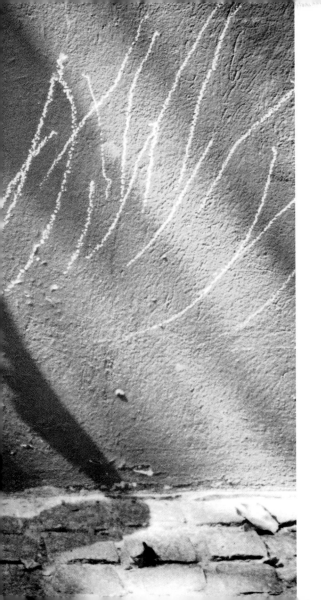

The Zen way of calligraphy
is to write in the most
straightforward, simple way
as if you were a beginner,
not trying to make something
skillful or beautiful, but simply
writing with full attention
as if you were discovering
what you were writing
for the first time;
then your full nature
would be in your writing.

—SHUNRYU SUZUKI

Hide yourself
in each and every thing.

—SOIKU SHIGEMATSU

Seeing

into

n o t h i n g n e s s —

this is the true seeing, the eternal seeing.

—SHEN HUI

In

the beginner's mind

there are many possibilities,

but in the expert's mind

there are

few.

—SHUNRYU SUZUKI

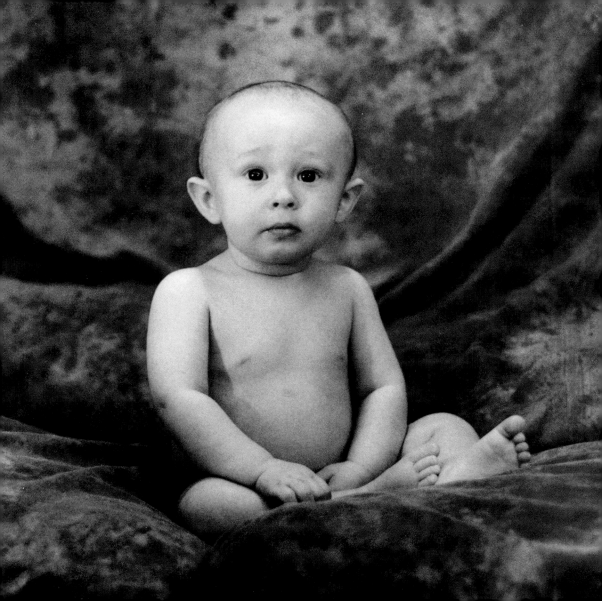

The journey of a thousand miles starts from beneath your feet. —ZEN SAYING, 365 ZEN

Fall seven times,

stand up eight.

—CHINESE PROVERB

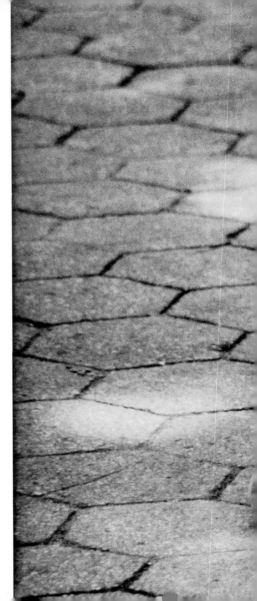

THIS IS IT

AND I AM IT

AND YOU ARE IT

AND SO IS THAT

AND HE IS IT

AND SHE IS IT

AND IT IS IT

AND THAT IS THAT.

—JAMES BROUGHTON

I think I think; therefore,

I think I am. —AMBROSE BIERCE

Handle even a *single* leaf of green

in such a way that it manifests the body

of the *Buddha*.

This in turn allows the Buddha to manifest

through the *leaf*.

—ZEN MASTER DOGEN

He who has found
and knows his soul
has found
all the world.

—THE UPANISHADS

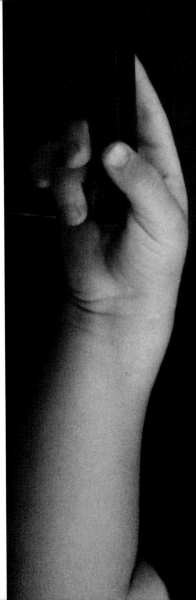

You cannot *talk* about apple juice to

someone who has not tasted it.

No matter what you say,

the other person will not have the

t r u e   e x p e r i e n c e of apple juice.

The only way is to *d r i n k   i t .*

—THICH NHAT HANH,
BE STILL AND KNOW

Trying to define yourself

is like trying to

bite your own teeth.

—ALAN WATTS

Life can be understood backward,

but must be lived *forward*.

—SØREN AABYE KIERKEGAARD

Except during the nine months

before he draws his first breath,

no man manages his affairs

as well as a tree does.

—GEORGE BERNARD SHAW

Zen

is to have the *heart* and S O U L

of a little child.

—TAKUAN SŌHŌ

It does not matter

how slowly you go

as long as you

do not stop.

—CONFUCIUS

See everyone as a Buddha.

—MASTER BAEK

In baseball, you don't know *nothing*.

—YOGI BERRA

At a given moment

I open my eyes and exist.

And before that, during all eternity,

what was there?

Nothing.

—UGO BETTI

EVERYTHING

comes to pass,

nothing

comes to stay.

—MATTHEW FLICKSTEIN,
JOURNEY TO THE CENTER

If you realize

you have enough,

you are truly rich.

—LAO TZU, *TAO TE CHING*

You have said what you are.

I am what I am.

—MEVLANA JALALUDDIN RUMI

Keep your hands o p e n ,

and all the sands of the desert can pass through them.

Close them, and all you can feel is a bit of

GRIT.

—TAISEN DESHIMARU

Thinking of human beings alone

is a bit narrow. To consider

that all sentient beings in

the universe have been our mother

at some point in time

opens a space of compassion.

—HIS HOLINESS
THE DALAI LAMA

Attain deliverance in disturbances.

—*A ZEN FOREST*

The sweetest flower in the world:

a baby's hands.

—ALGERNON CHARLES SWINBURNE

Before you study Zen,
a bowl is a bowl and tea is tea.

While you are studying Zen,
a bowl is no longer a bowl and tea is no longer tea.

After you've studied Zen,
a bowl is again a bowl and tea is tea.

—ZEN SAYING

EVERYONE

IS IN THE

BEST SEAT.

—JOHN CAGE

Come out of the circle of time and into the circle of love.

—MEVLANA JALALUDDIN RUMI

Harm no other beings,

they are only

your brothers and sisters.

—BUDDHA

Every baby born into the world

is a *finer* one than the last.

—CHARLES DICKENS

I don't know,

I don't care,

and it doesn't make

any difference.

—JACK KEROUAC

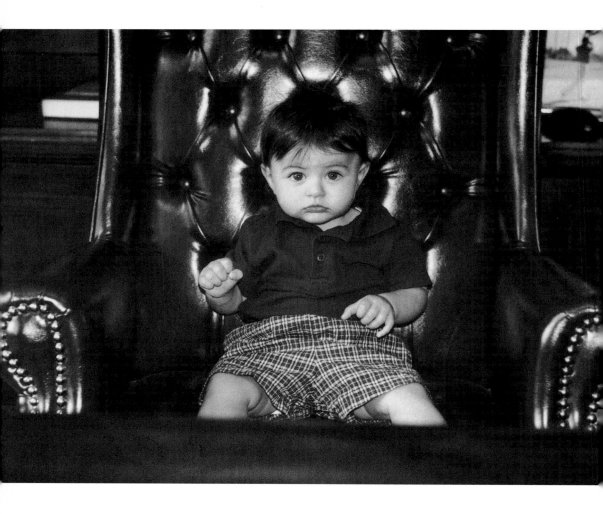

The master doesn't talk, he acts.

—LAO TZU, *TAO TE CHING*

Stay centered,

do not overstretch.

Extend from your center,

return to your center.

—JACK KORNFIELD,
*BUDDHA'S LITTLE
INSTRUCTION BOOK*

To RECEIVE everything,

one must open one's hands and *give*.

—TAISEN DESHIMARU

Their souls dwell

in the house of tomorrow,

which you cannot visit, not even

in your dreams . . .

for life goes not backward nor tarries

with yesterday.

—KAHLIL GIBRAN

Are there none so **wise** to learn

from the E X P E R I E N C E of others?

—ZEN SAYING

Just realize where you come from.

This is the essence of wisdom.

—LAO TZU,
TAO TE CHING

PHOTOGRAPHS

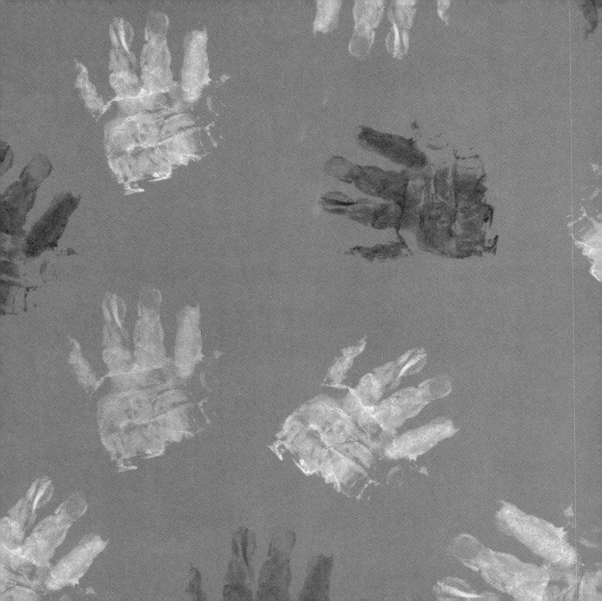